This colourin book belong to:
Este libro de colorear pertenece a :

....

....

....

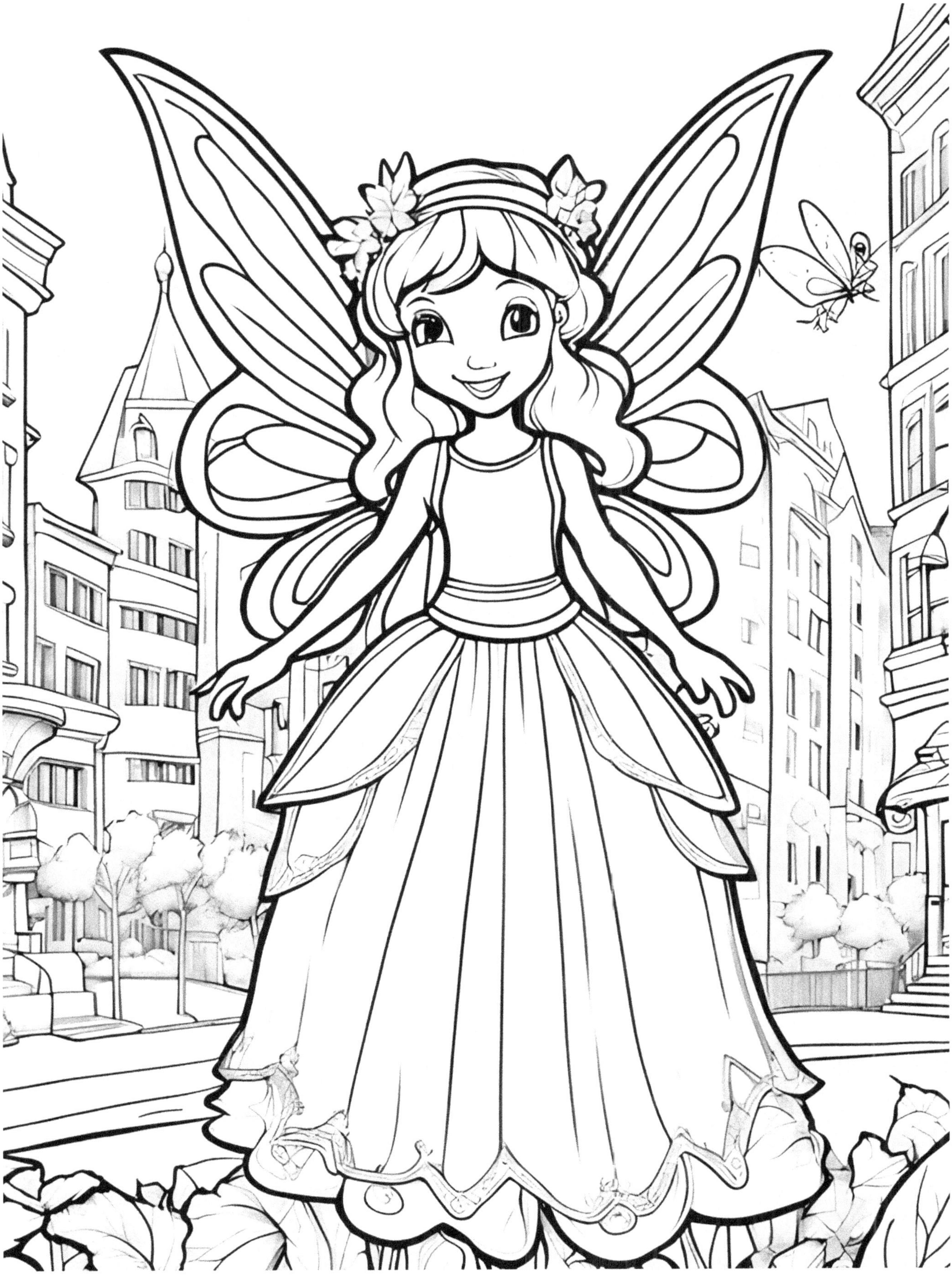

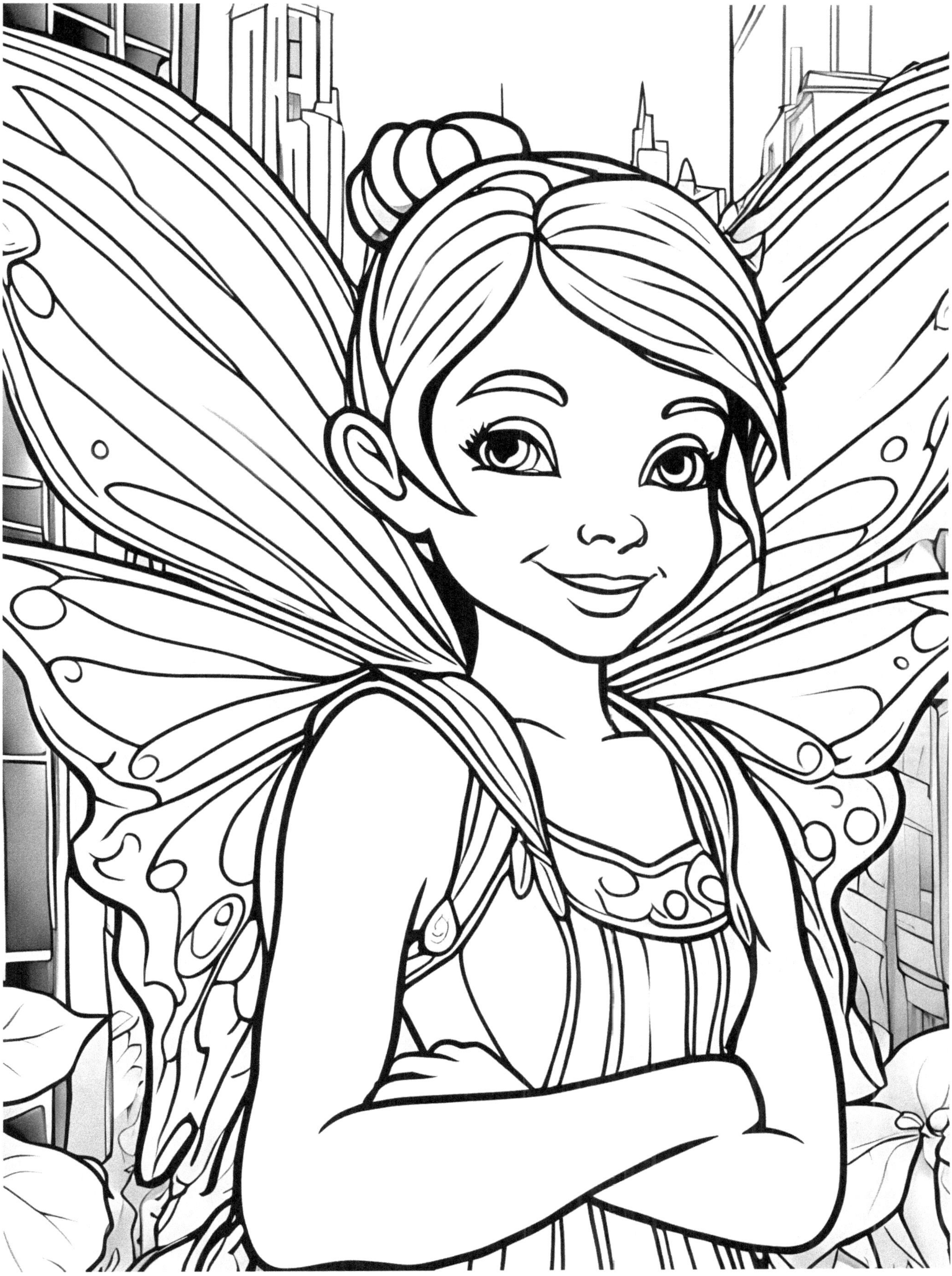

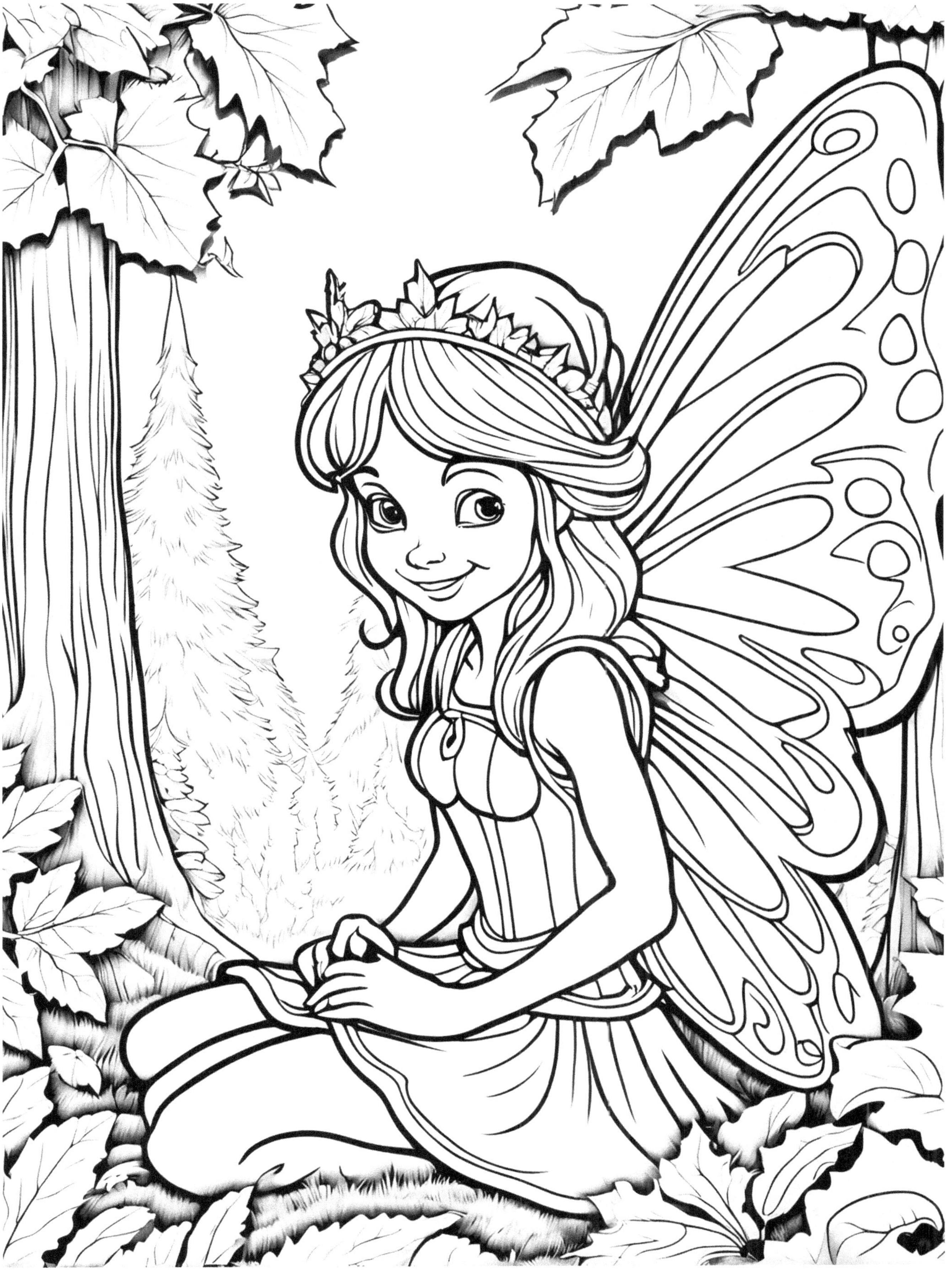

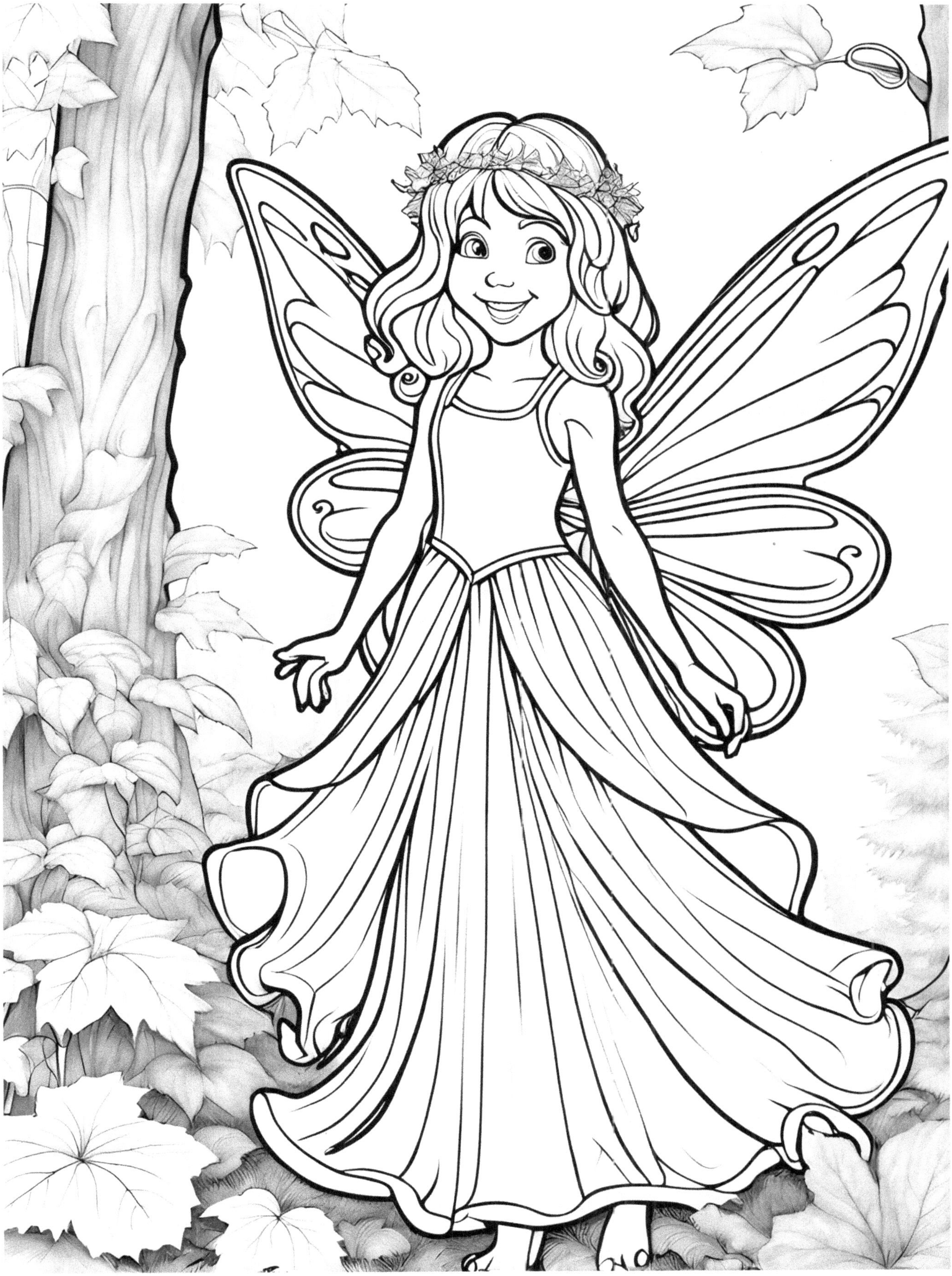

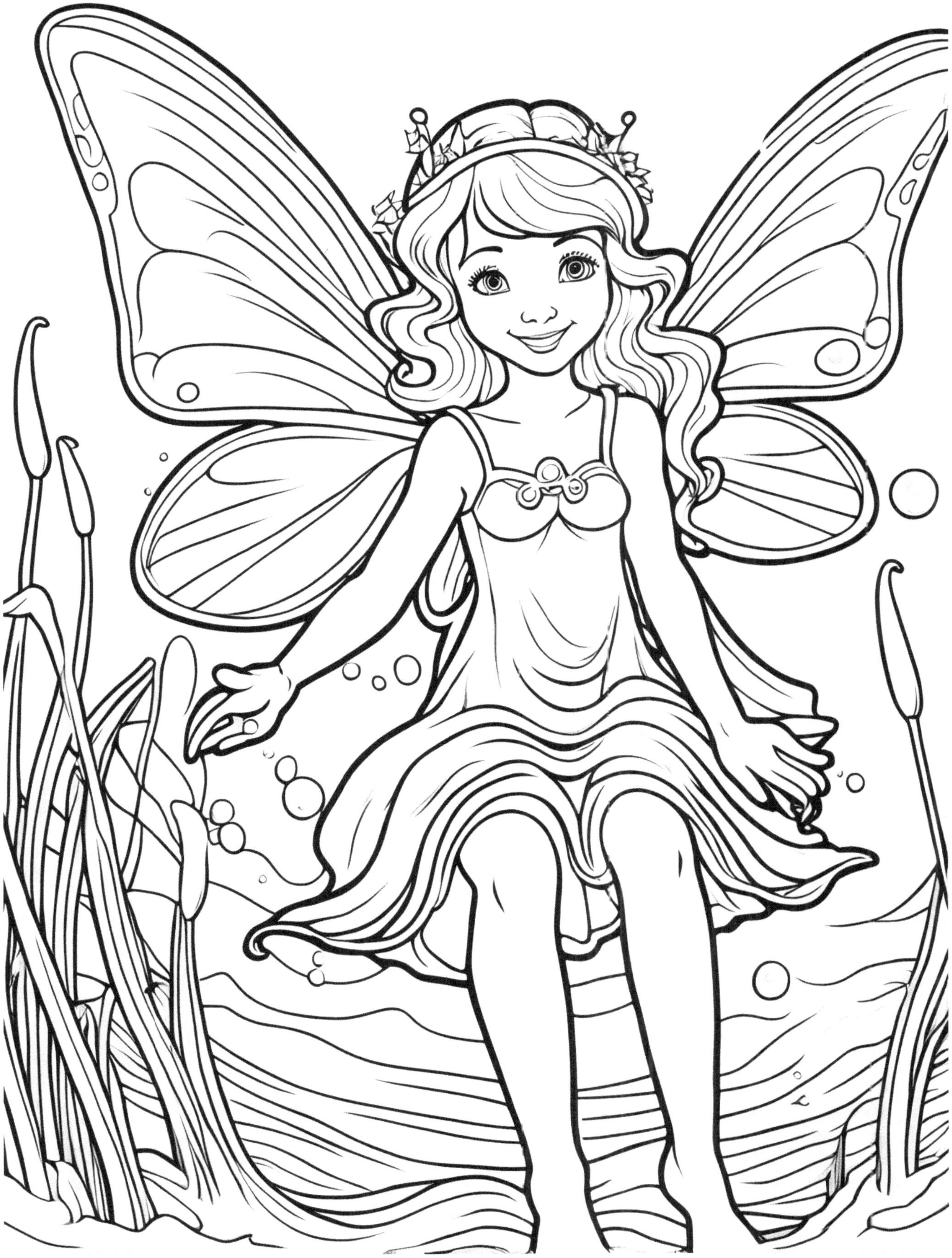

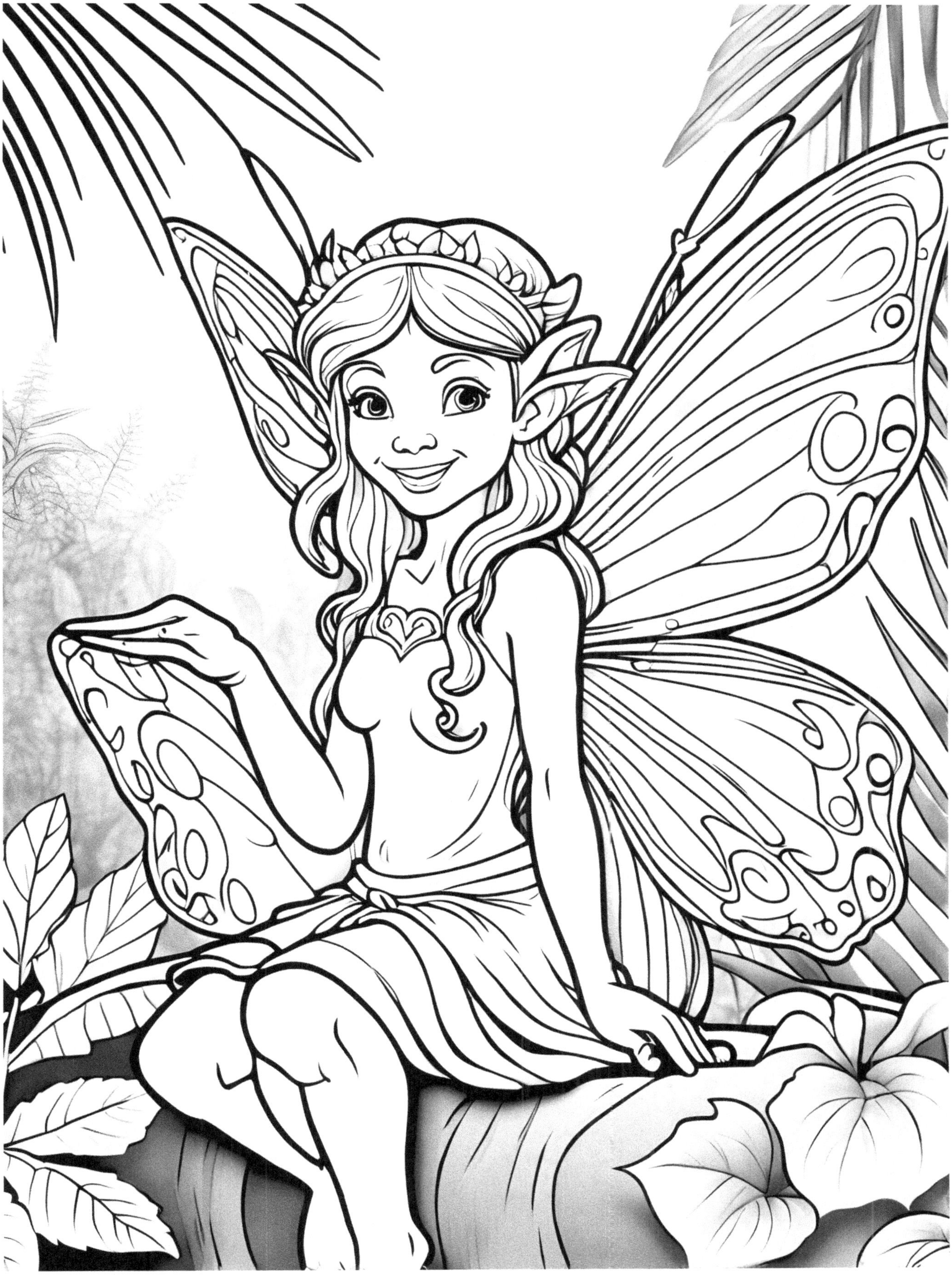

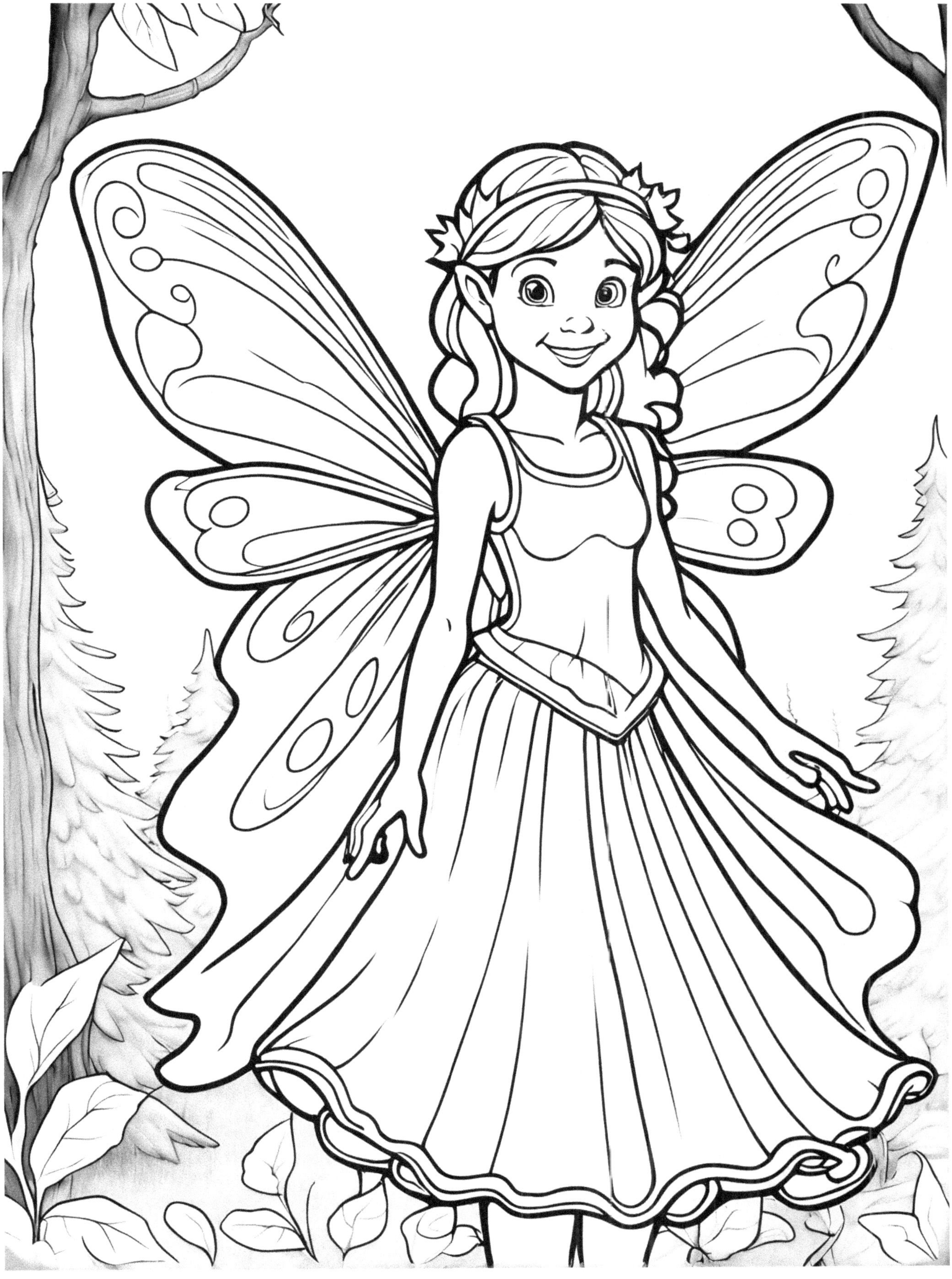

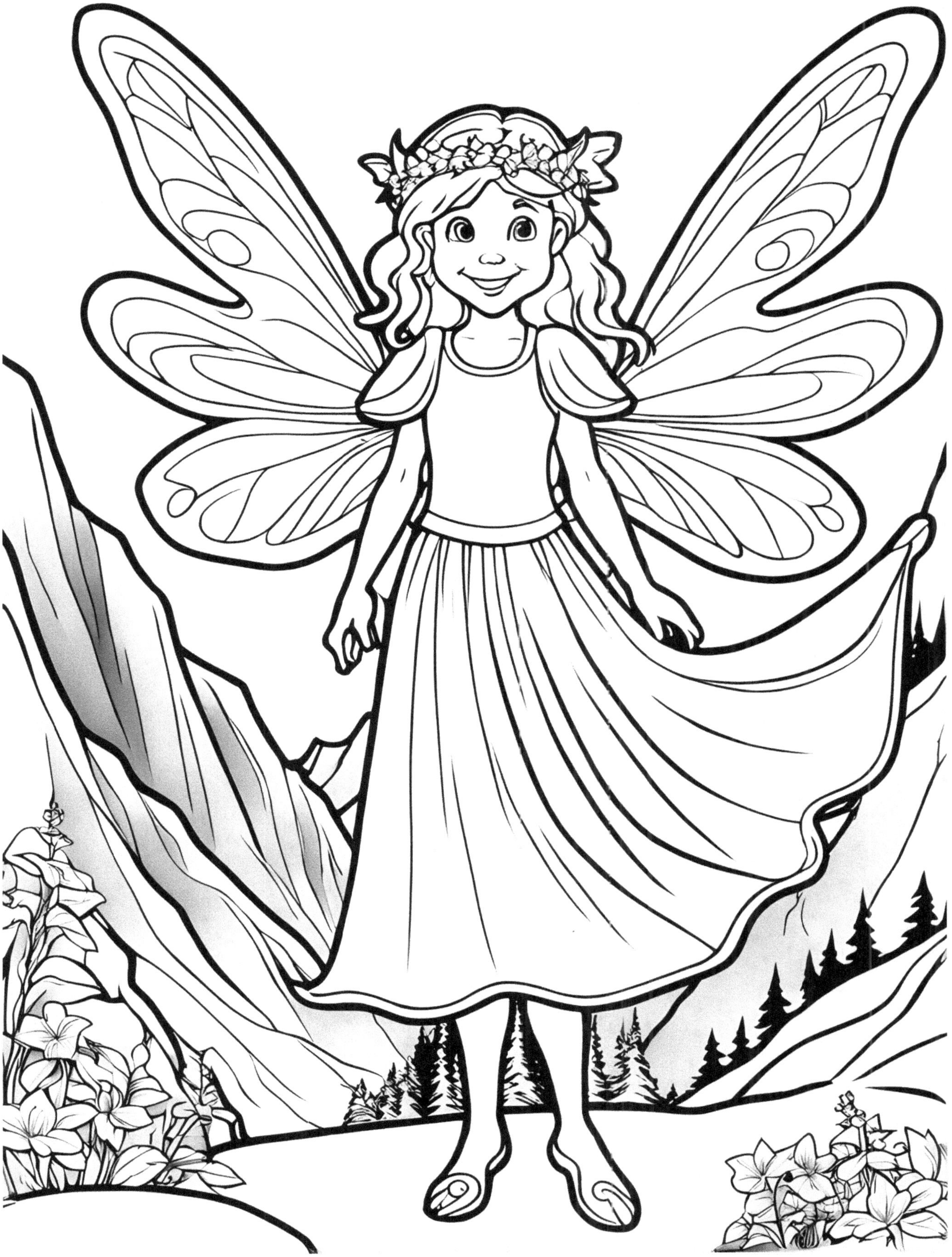

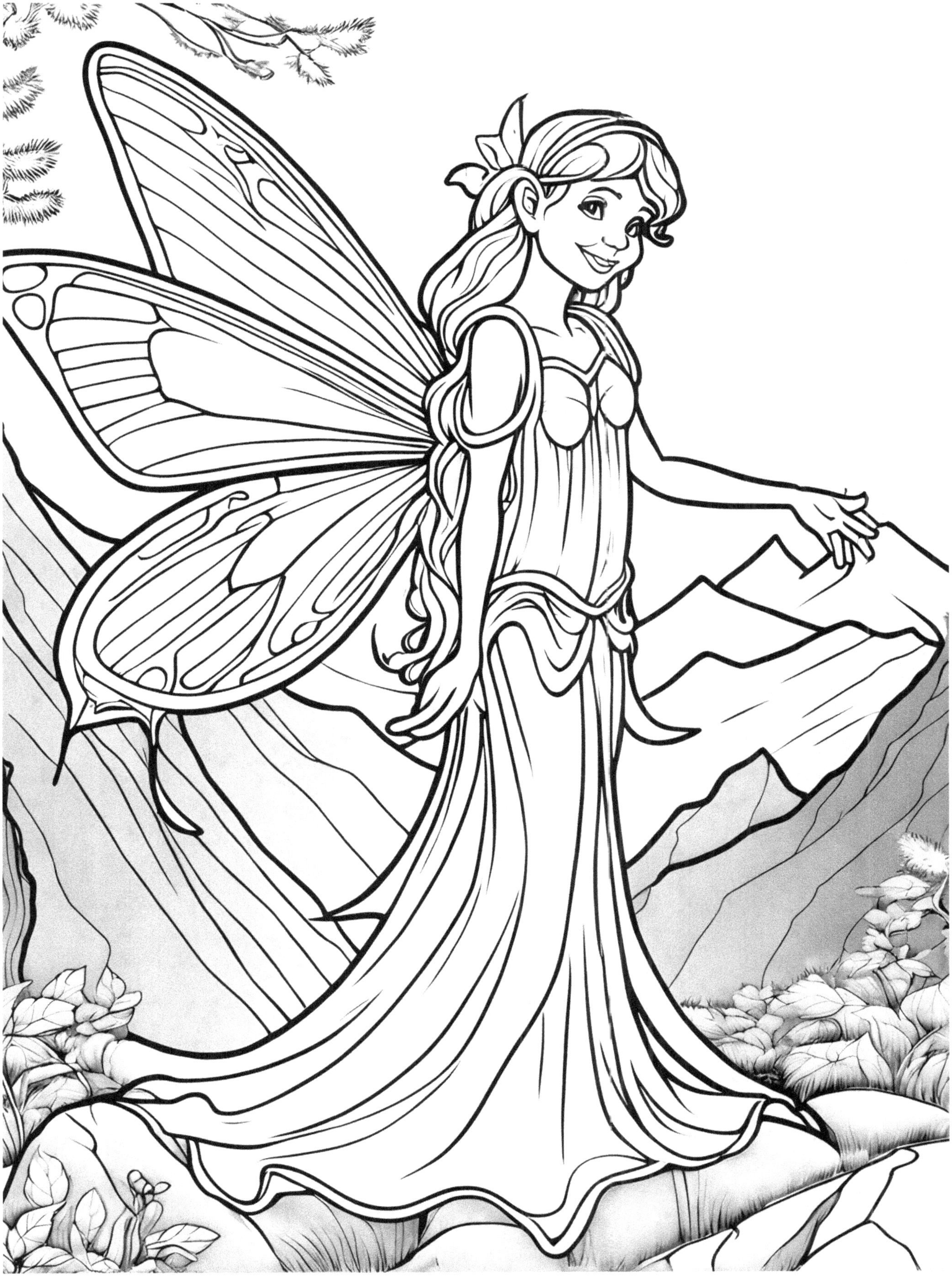

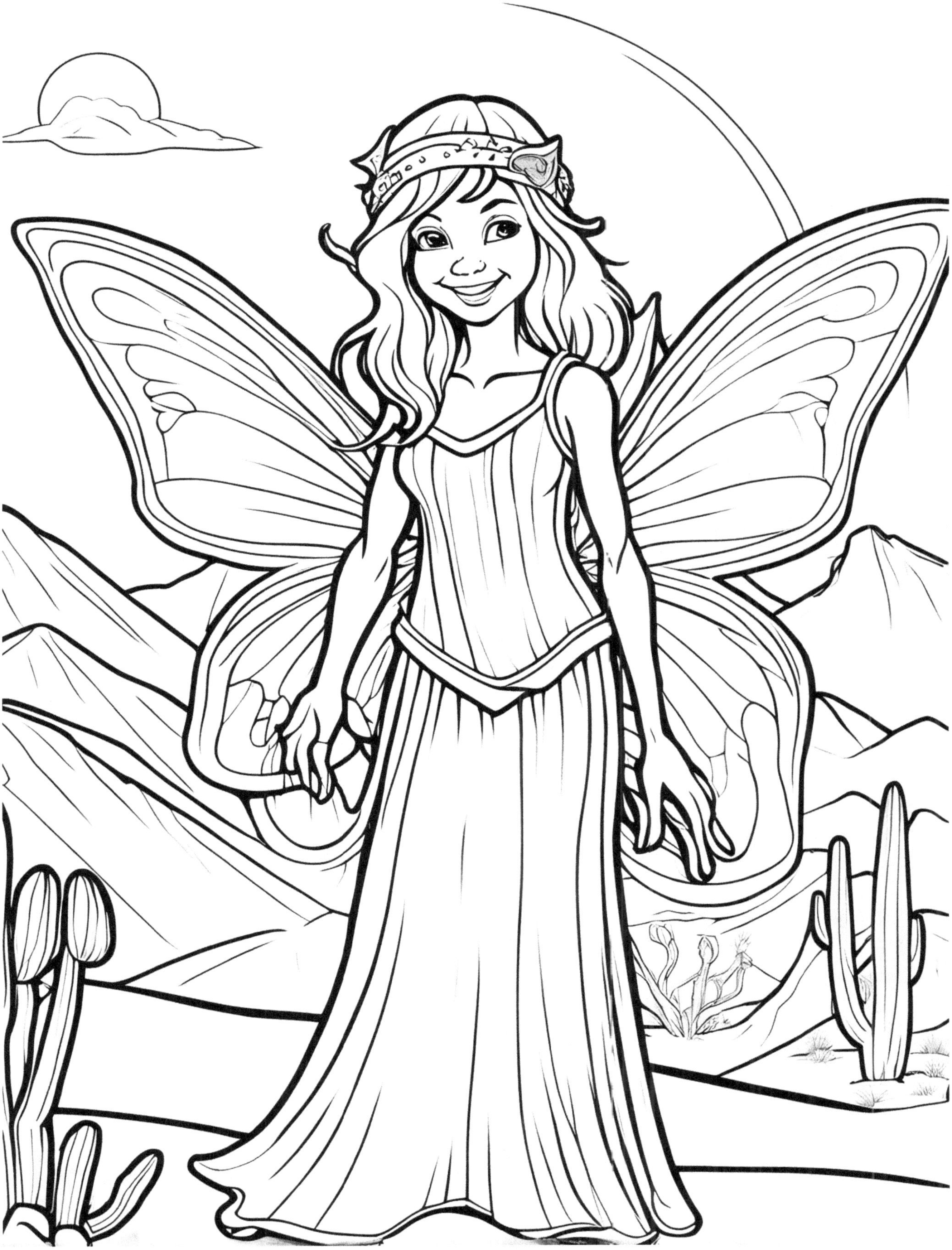

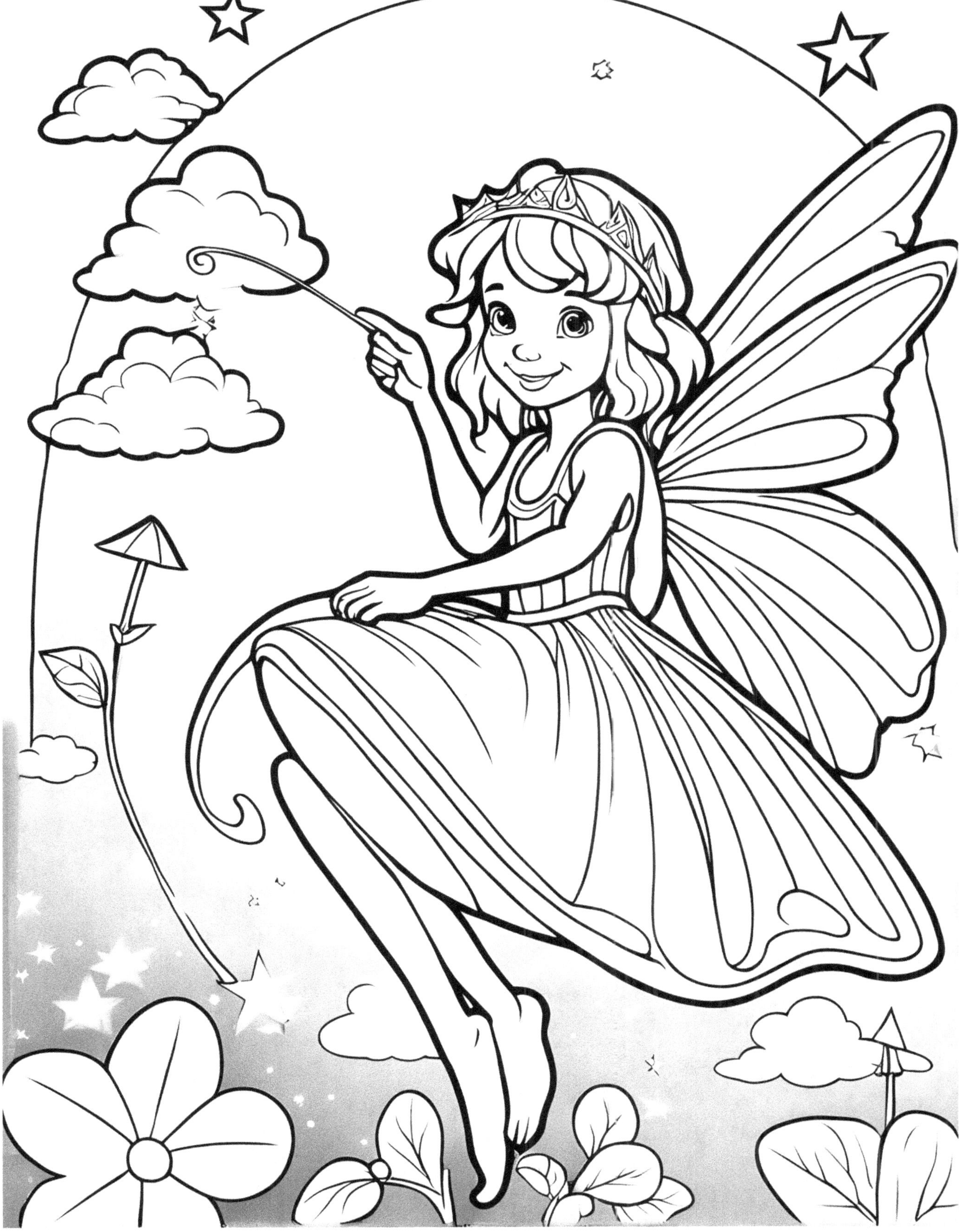

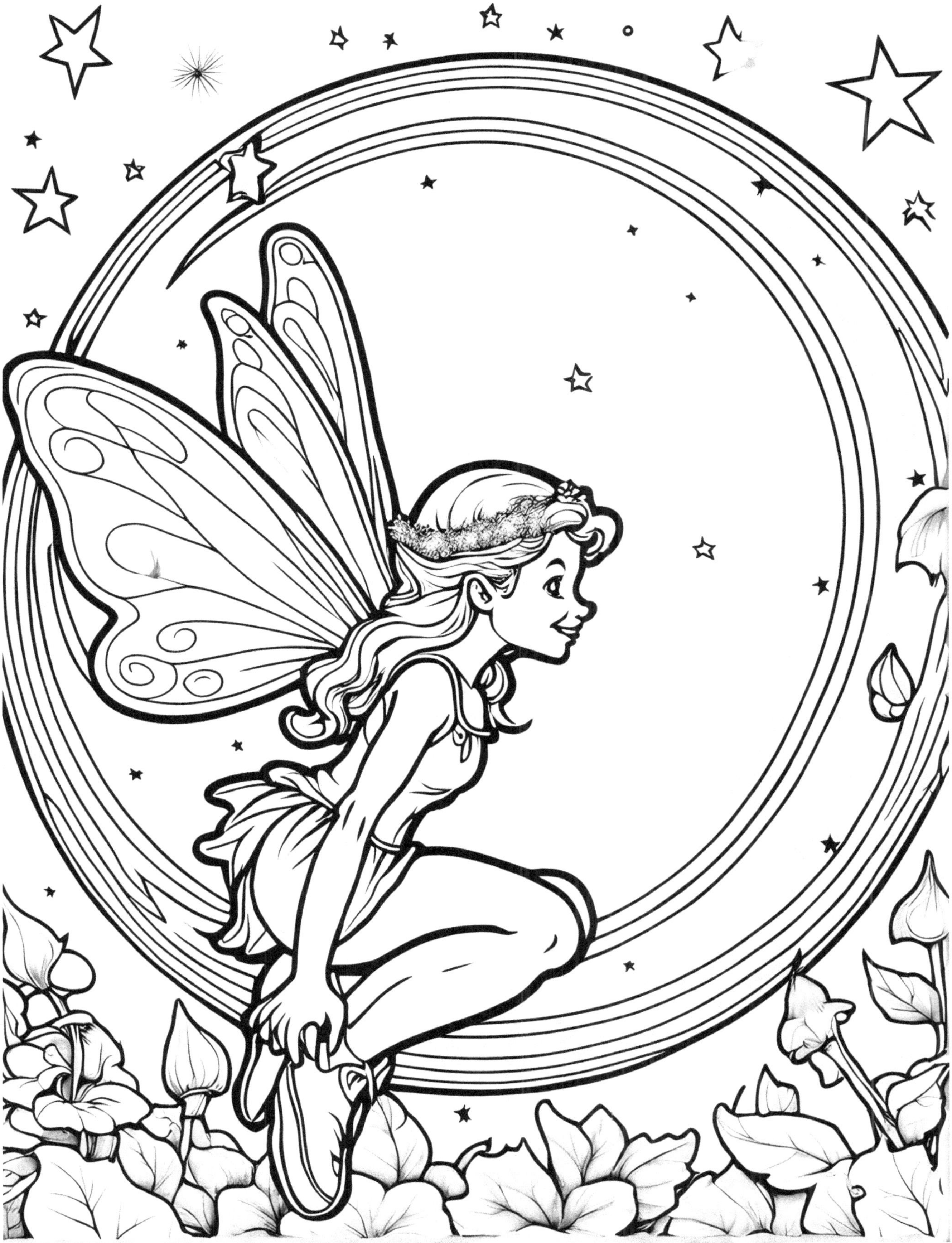

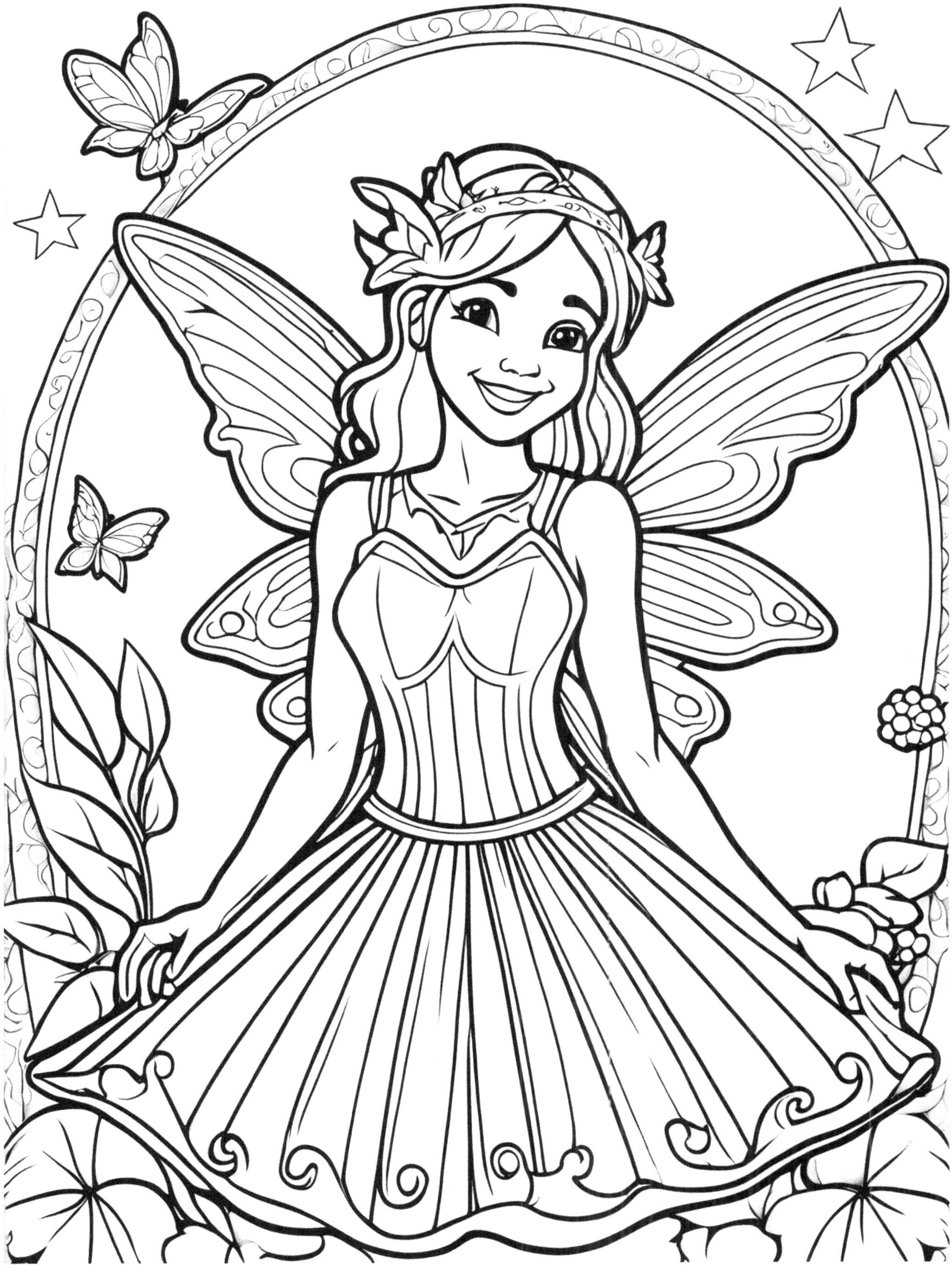

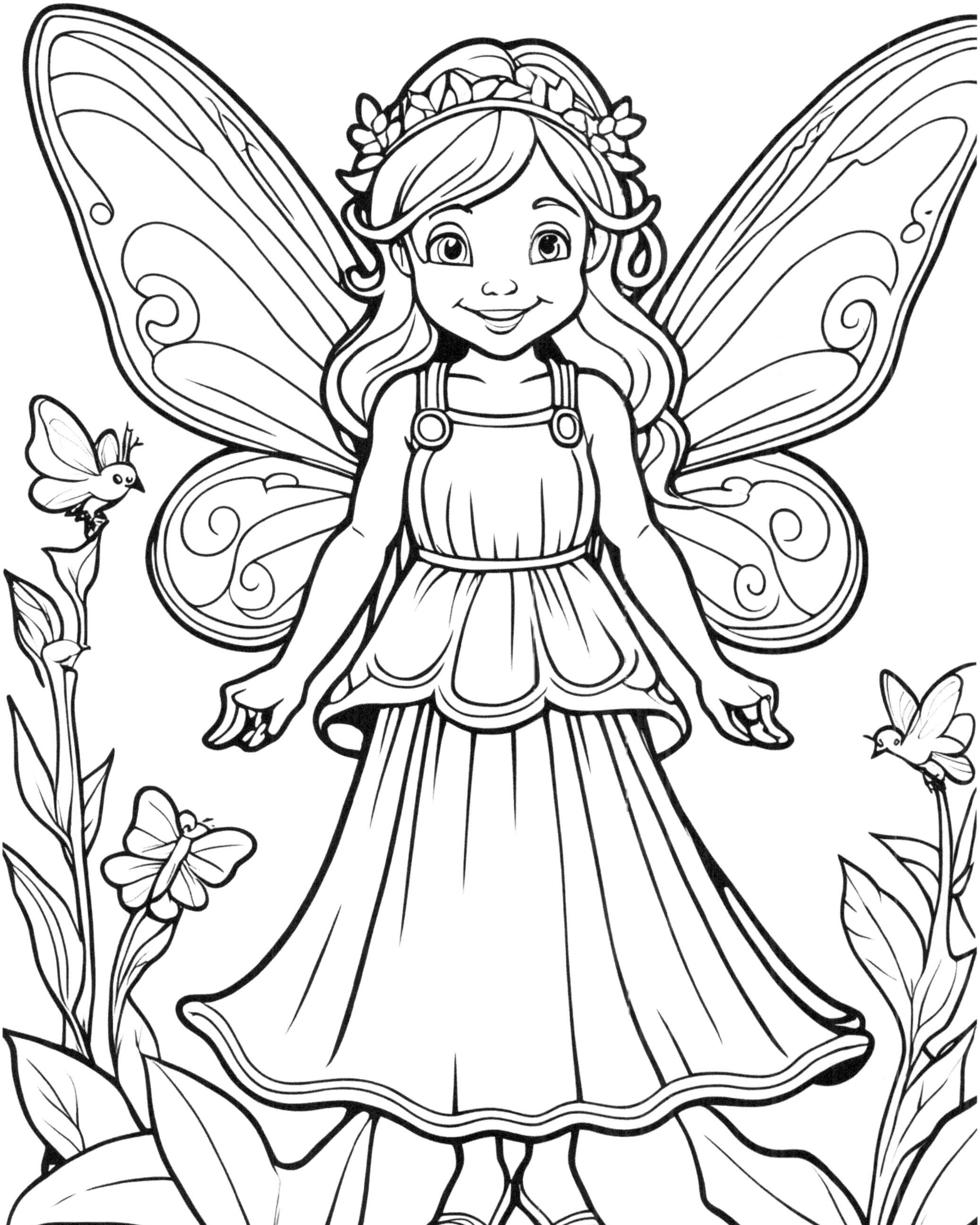

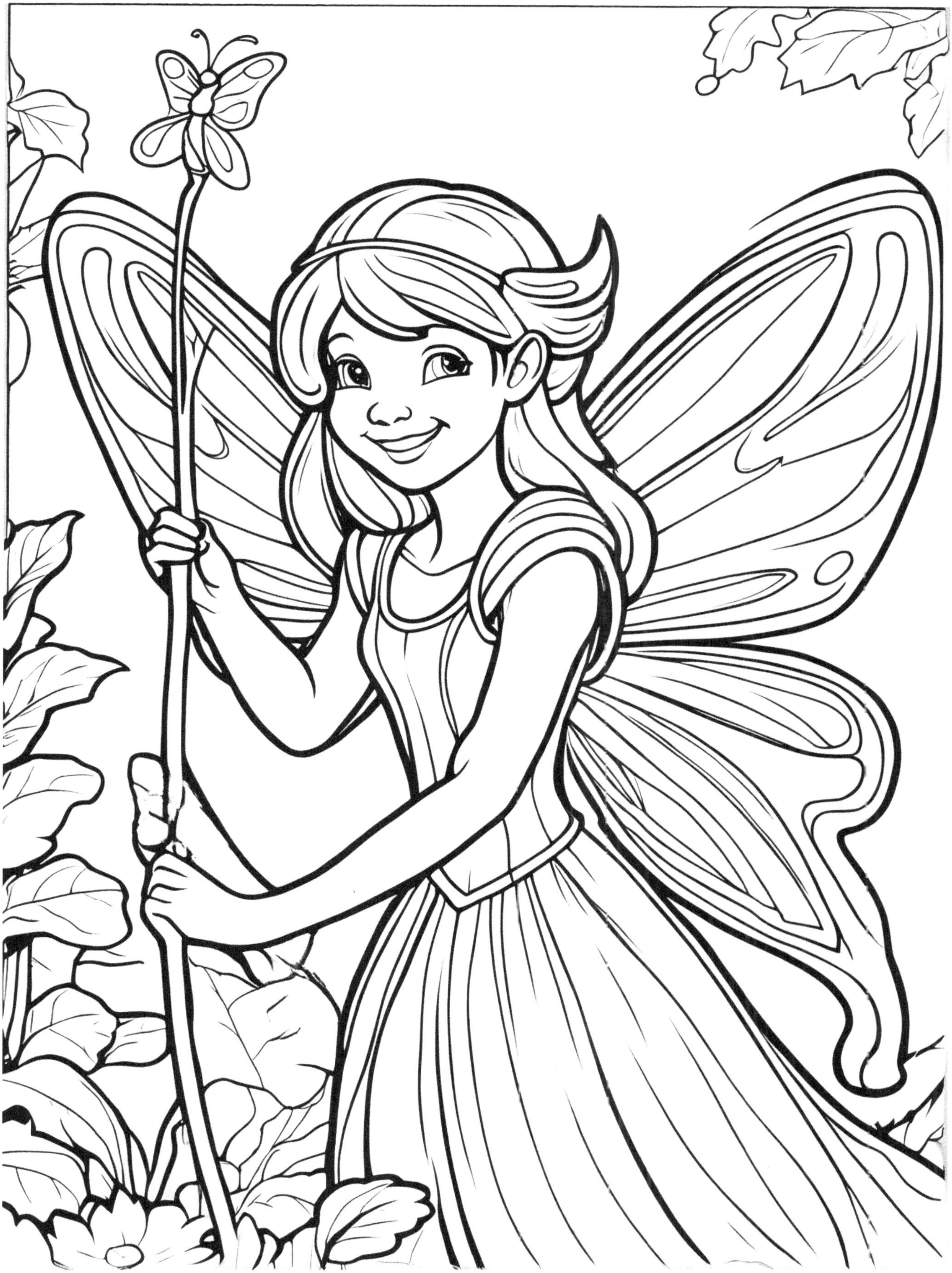

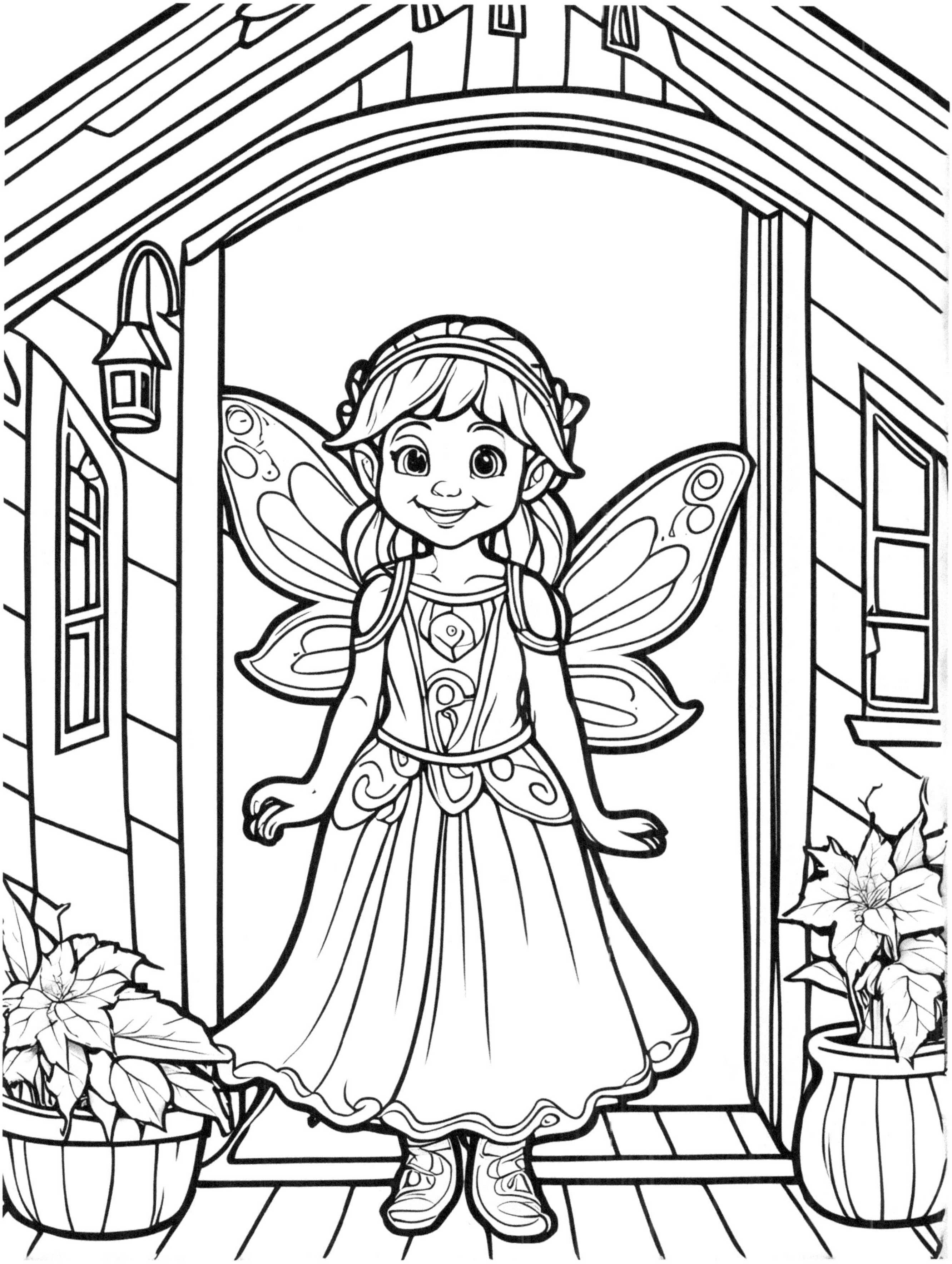

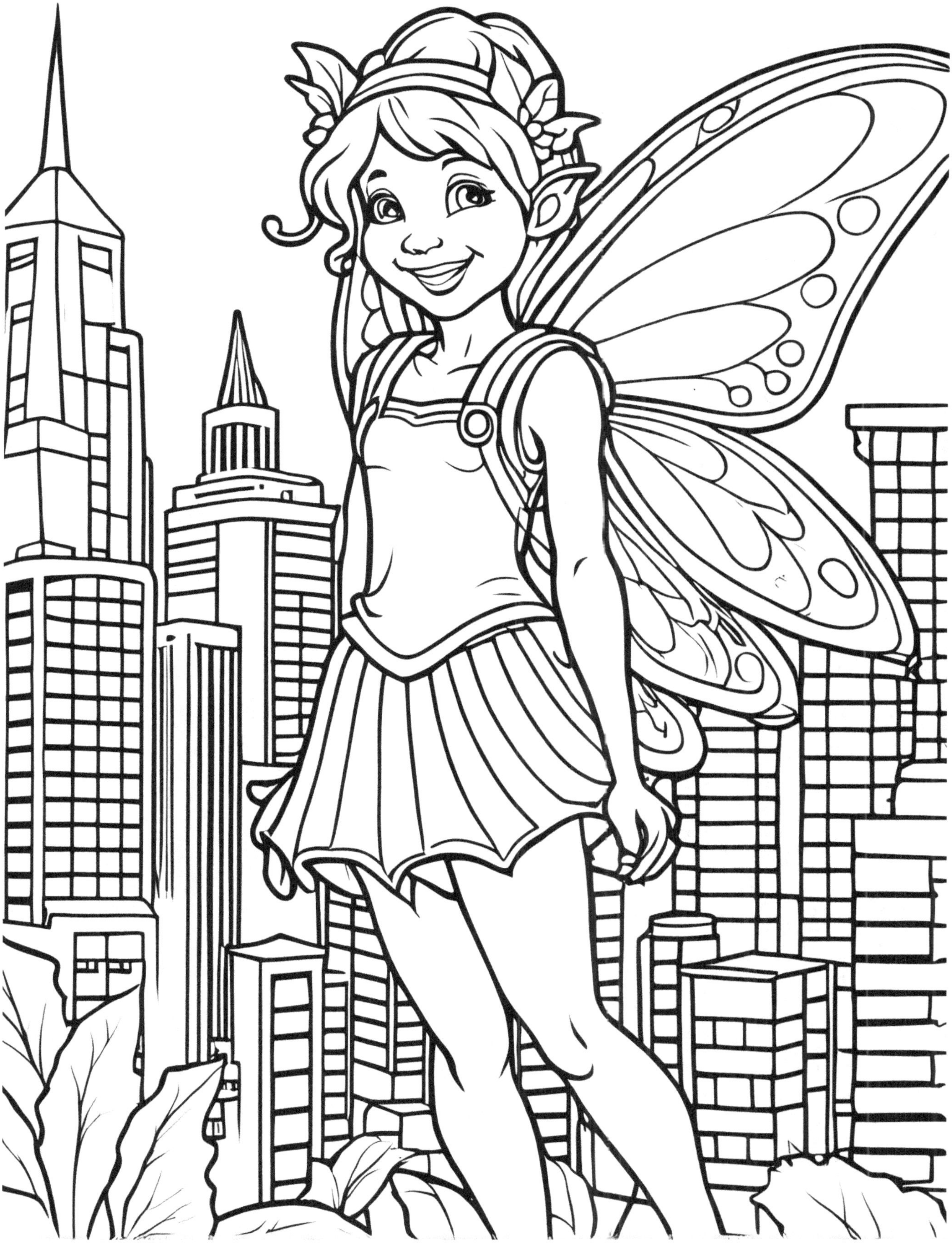

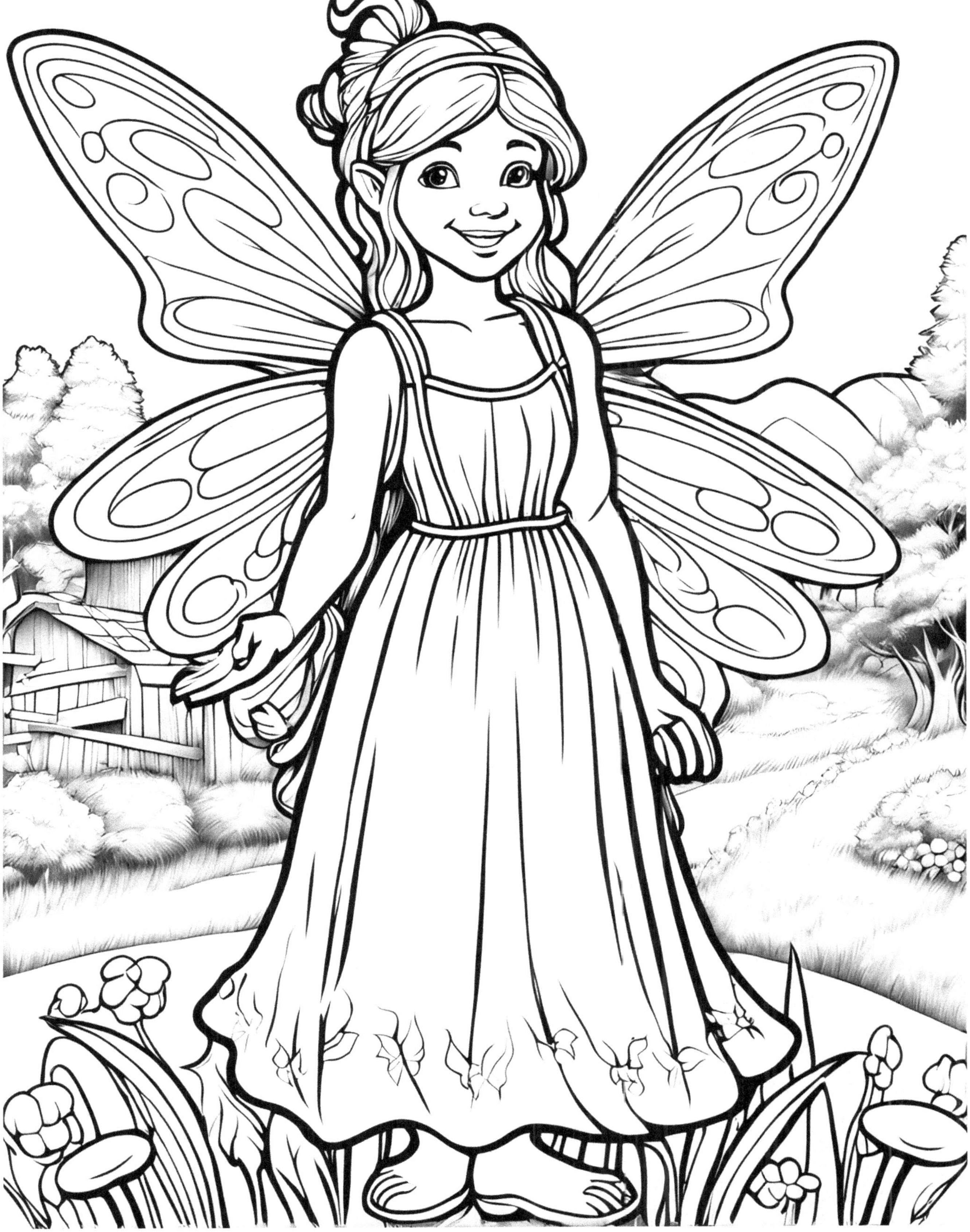

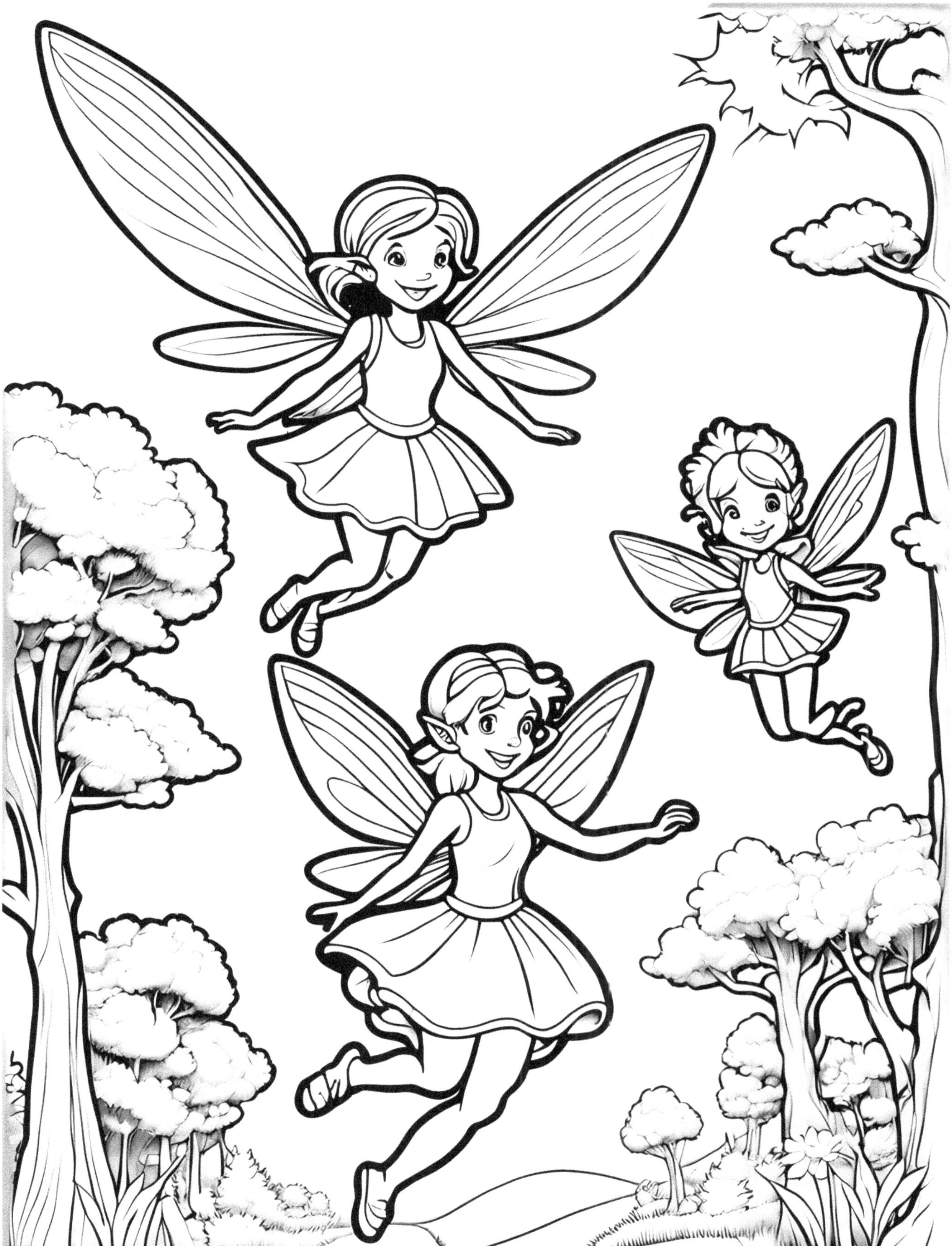

www.ingramcontent.com/pod-product-compliance
Lightning Source LLC
Chambersburg PA
CBHW082201290526
45794CB00008B/3375
9798860278479